I0468405

Becoming Rich In 42 Days:
The Step By Step Method To Make Money Online And Live Your Dreams Starting From Scratch.

Copyright © 2016, Remy Roulier

TABLE OF CONTENTS

I- INTRODUCTION.

Just imagine ...

... Not having a boss on your back.

... Becoming completely financially independent, and never be afraid of running out of money to pay your bills.

... Having more time for you, your family and your passions.

... Being able to finally live your dreams instead of just dreaming your life.

This is now possible by working on the Internet.

And the benefits of working on the web don't not stop here.

You'll also get what even a great wage could never offer you: **the luxury of geographical independence**.

The goal of this method is to give you a "turnkey" method to acquire your financial independence by working on the Internet, from anywhere in the world.

The strategies you will discover here actually work and are the ones I have been using for a long time to make a living on the Internet, far much better than I could have ever hoped to earn when I was working for companies first as a computer science engineer and later as a marketing manager.

And the other crucial difference is that now I'm free to live my dreams and travel anywhere in the world.

Many people did it. I did it. Now it's your turn to do it.

And it is possible in just 42 days. So take action now!

II- CHOOSING YOUR NICHE MARKET (7 DAYS).

II.1- The Contrarian Process.

In a classical process of creating a product, people first create the product, then "push" their product towards the customer. Then, they cross their fingers and hope he would buy the product if by chance it matches his needs, at least partially.

This strategy is very limited because it focuses on the product and not on the real needs of the customer, and you are not sure that your product will sell and will interest someone.

The contrarian process does the exact opposite of the classical process.

This process will first identify a niche market in which people have a real need, then create a product that will exactly match the needs that people have, and that will give them the perfect solution.

This strategy is much more rewarding and ensures that your product will sell without having to cross your fingers because it will answer the questions and solve the problems people really have.

So you will want to use the contrarian process to create your product.

Starting from people's need, create the product that exactly meets this need, and sell that product being sure it will sell like hotcakes.

II.2- The Two Essential Requirements To Choose Your Niche.

Before creating your product, you will have to find a niche market in which to create it, and above all to choose a niche that will be profitable.

Hence the importance of choosing your niche market. If you choose it the wrong way, all the efforts you spent creating your product might be vain because your product will not sell at all or too little to ensure you enough income.

That is why to be profitable, the niche market you choose must absolutely meet these two following conditions.

II.2.a- Choosing a hungry niche market.

The first condition is to choose a hungry niche market. In other words, a niche market where there is a group of people having a particular need, a common problem they want to solve at all costs.

A little bit like a group of starving lions that are waiting for someone to throw them a good chunk of meat.

So, you are going to target a group of people with a common specific need, a problem they are desperately trying to solve.

The more important their problem will be, the more your product that will solve their problem will be wanted, and the more you will be able to sell it at a high price.

Problems can be classified in two main categories:

The Major Problems.

These are all problems that poison your customers' lives and make their life hell.

Among the major problems we can find serious debt problems, family problems, weight problems, health problems, smoking issues, etc.

Products that solve such problems literally change the lives of your customers, that's why they are ready to pay a very high price to get them.

So, these types of products are by far the most profitable but on the other hand you will have to face a very tough competition.

The Secondary Problems.

These problems are least important to solve and relate to a secondary desire.

For example: learning to swim, playing the piano, using a design software, etc.

If you are a beginner, I highly recommend you to start with this type of products.

These products are less profitable than those who solve a major problem, but you can much more easily beat your competitors if your marketing is good.

The creation of a product will also be much easier for you. Simply take a topic you like or know (playing the piano, using a photo editing software, maintaining a vegetable garden etc.), and you will not necessarily need to make a lot of research to create a quality product.

Furthermore, I highly recommend you to find a problem that is not related to a temporary trend but that will still exist even after several years.

This will ensure you that your product will still sell well in five or ten years because the need will always exist.

Indeed, you're more likely to sell for years a method teaching how to learn the guitar rather than a method to understand the latest features of the iPhone 6.

The first method will never become outdated you will continue to sell it very well even in thirty years, while the second will be obsolete in six months and your sales volume will decrease drastically.

Before going further, I recommend you to list about 20 of your personal problems and desires, especially those you managed to solve or managed to get rid of.

These 20 problems must now pass the second filter, which is to satisfy the second condition for a profitable niche market.

II.2.b- Choosing a niche market that is big enough.

The **second requirement** for a profitable niche market is to make sure that **your niche market is big enough**.

It is necessary that the group of people having the problem that your product will solve be large enough to ensure an important sales volume.

If your product solves the problem that only a tiny group of ten persons have, don't expect to make a lot of money with that.

At best you will make ten sales, assuming that no competitor before you sold them his product.

However, if your product solves the problem of ten thousand or a hundred thousand people, then you greatly increase your chances of making a large volume of sales. Although there is competition, there is a good chance that there is room for everyone.

A good way to know if a niche market is big enough is to use the free tool Google Adwords Keyword Planner (https://adwords.google.com/KeywordPlanner).

This tool will let you know the monthly number of times users are searching for a specific keyword or phrase on Google.

You can target this search worldwide, on one country, one city or even one language.

The tool also gives you for each keyword and phrase an idea of the competition (a column indicates whether competition is low, medium or high).

The best is of course to find keywords that people search a lot and who have no or very little competition.

However, these "golden nuggets" are very rare to find.

So it's ok to find keywords or phrases that are highly searched and where competition is average.

Now start using Keyword Planner and compare the keywords related to the product ideas you listed before.

Choose the product ideas that have the highest monthly searches and the less competition.

An interesting number of monthly searches starts from several thousand, ideally from 8000-10000.

If searches are less than 1000 or 2000, think carefully before you choose this product idea. Remember, the goal is to sell a lot and in the long term.

Another good complementary way to ensure that your product idea is not only a temporary trend and that the need will be durable is to use Google Trends tool (https://www.google.com/trends/).

This tool allows you to have a history of the number of searches on a given keyword.

This way, you can see if the theme is stable or increases over time or if it's related to a short-term trend that will not last or that is decreasing.

If you have correctly done the steps above, you should have found one or more profitable niche markets.

Now, you have one or more product ideas that will answer a real need of your customers, and this need concerns a large enough number of people to ensure you a significant sales volume.

Moreover, the competition should not be too high and you'll be able to sell these products for many years because they do not depend on a temporary trend.

Now, let's see how to create your product.

III- CREATING YOUR PRODUCT (14 DAYS).

III.1- Choosing The Right Format For Your Product.

The first thing to think about before creating your product is to **choose a product** that is both **quickly reproducible** and at a **minimal manufacturing cost**.

III.1.a- A product that is quickly reproducible.

Any business, no matter its size, has three distinct areas of activity: execution, management, and leadership.

Execution consists in performing the tasks and daily tasks related to your business. It's your heart of business: changing the circuit breakers for an electrician, programming a software for a developer, writing articles for a blogger.

Management is the organization and the planning of these missions and tasks.

Finally, leadership is the strategic work done to develop your business and your sales (new products or services, new distribution channels, optimizing the business that already exists etc.).

To really grow, we must minimize the time spent at execution, in order to focus on management and leadership.

Hence the importance of having a product that can be reproduced quickly, to spend a minimum amount of time at execution.

This is not the case if you are selling for example hand-made lamps where each lamp takes you two hours to create. Assuming you work eight hours a day, you know in advance that you could sell only four lamps per day maximum, which limits your turnover. In addition, you have no more time left for management and leadership: your business can not grow.

It's the same thing if you provide services. An electrician who has ten appointments per day can not plan others appointments since he does not have any time left. His turnover can not increase, and he has no time to think about his business development strategy.

However, if part of the execution of lamps is outsourced or if the electrician hires an employee, then there it will create more time to spend on management and leadership.

That's why you need ideally a product that is both infinitely and instantly reproducible.

In this case your business has no more limits and you can focus as much as you want on management and leadership, and you can sell as many copies as you have customers.

III.1.b- A product with a minimum manufacturing cost.

It seems pretty obvious that the less expensive your product is in terms of manufacturing costs, and the more important your margin will be.

Ideally, you will want to have a product that costs you nothing or almost nothing to produce or reproduce, and sell it at a price at least ten times higher to what it costs you to produce.

This way, you will be able to invest in advertising and generate profits, even in competitive fields.

For example, if your product does not cost you even a dollar to produce and that you sell it $37, it gives you an incredible flexibility to spend tens of dollars in advertising to get a customer.

Buying as much advertising guarantees you to easily sell your product, even without having optimized your sales page or your ads (we will see this in details in the next chapters).

Thus, there is a product format that gathers all these benefits: quickly reproducible and with minimal manufacturing costs.

These are the digital products.

They can be reproduced both infinitely and instantly, leaving you plenty of time to focus on management and leadership.

They cost nothing to produce, which allows to have the highest possible margin of benefits.

By digital products we mean: digital books or ebooks, video products (eg mp4), audio products (eg mp3), web applications, online trainings in a members area, softwares, smartphone apps, plugins etc.

So for all these reasons, I highly recommend you to choose this kind of format (digital products).

Now, take the product idea that you found in the previous chapter and select which digital format you will use to create your product (text, audio, video, etc.).

If you absolutely do not want a digital format, an alternative would be to choose physical media such as paper books or DVDs.

Should you choose between a paper book or a DVD, I recommend you a DVD. It takes a lot less time to create than a paper book, costs almost nothing to produce (around one dollar for the box, the cover and the plastic film), and it has a much higher perceived value than a book. It can also be sold at a higher price than a book.

Now, let's see the different methodologies to create your product in the format you chose here.

We are going to start with digital products and see how to create a ebook, a video product, an audio product, a web application, an online training and other types of digital products.

Then we will see the additional steps to put your digital product on a physical medium, either paper or CD / DVD.

III.2- How To Create An Ebook.

Let's break the myth of the digital book: you do not need to be a writing expert to create a quality ebook.

You can manage to do it by being as you are, with the knowledge you have now. And if you are not sure of your abilities, remember that bestsellers are not necessarily the best written books.

First we will see how many words your ebook should have, then how long it takes to create it.

Then you will see a seven-step method to create your book in a minimum amount of time and also to maximize the quality of your content.

III.2.a- Size of your ebook.

The size of a digital book is variable.

In our case, the ebook will be a practical ebook. In other words, it will bring a solution to a problem that your customers have. In this sense, the size of your book has no real meaning, since your customers will judge the quality of your book on its ability to solve their problem, not on its length.

Moreover, many people will prefer a short book that is straight to the point and provides a clear solution, rather than a long but very rough book where they lose their time reading between the lines.

Thus, an interesting number of pages for your book is between 80 to 150 pages, but it's absolutely not a problem if your book only has 50 or even 40 pages, as far as your content provides an effective solution.

A practical ebook of over 200 pages starts to be too long. Remember that people will also choose your book because it saves them the time to search by themselves for the solution to their problem. So, you will not help them by writing additional sentences just to make your book look longer.

III.2.b- Time to write a digital book.

The time for writing an ebook is also variable.

You can easily write an ebook in a week to ten days if you are working fulltime on it every day.

It can also take you four times more time to write the same ebook if instead of writing one hour per day you write fifteen minutes per day.

Or you can also choose to create a book every three months by writing a little bit every day. Indeed, you only need to write two pages per day to create a book of 180 pages in three months.

In fact, the real question to ask yourself is not how much time you need to spend to write your book, but to decide **in how much time you want your book to be finished**.

Indeed, you have to know that the brain acts within the limits you set, and that the more time you have to do a work, the more time you will take, often unnecessarily.

For example, if you give yourself two hours to do a job, it is likely that you will fully use these two hours.

If you give yourself three hours for the same job, you will probably spend three hours.

However, if you decide in how much time you want to finish your book, then you take control over your time and you fully mobilize your resources to achieve this goal in due time (by setting of course realistic objectives and not trying to write 100 pages in 3 minutes...).

Moreover, the work will often be of better quality in less time because you will focus more easily, you will not allow yourself to be distracted and you will automatically go straight to the point.

Thus, depending on your motivation to quickly finish your book, you will be able to find more or less time each day to meet the deadline you have set, exactly as you do to meet the deadlines your boss sets if you are employed. The difference is that here: you're the boss!

Now, let's see a seven-step method to create your book step by step, that will allow you to spend a minimum amount of time and to maximize the quality of your content.

III.2.c- STEP 1: Create your table of contents.

You first need to know what exactly you are going to write. For that, you need a plan that will be your table of contents.

You will find in the next pages three different approaches to create a relevant table of contents, and of course you can mix these approaches to make the most of them.

1st Approach: Chronological table of contents.

You can make a table of contents based on the different steps or stages required to implement the solution you offer.

For example, if your book is about the creation of a Japanese garden in thirty days, you can make a table of contents in thirty short chapters, each chapter developing a step to create the Japanese garden.

The same way, if your book is about how to stop smoking in four weeks, you can make a table of contents segmented into four chapters (week 1, week 2, week 3 and week 4), with a specific theme for each week that will lead to completely eliminate the cigarette at the end of the fourth week.

You may need to add sub points if the time frame is too large.

For example, you can segment the first week in seven sub-points corresponding to the seven days of the week.

You can also segment the first week in three sub-points. The first sub-point would correspond to Monday, Tuesday, Wednesday, the second to Thursday, Friday, Saturday and the third to Sunday.

2nd Approach: Logical table of contents.

Here, there is no more an idea of time segmentation.

The goal is to create your table of contents based on your common sense and experience to find the different steps that must be performed in a logical order and step-by-step to gradually achieve the promised solution.

For example, if your book is about how to go out with a woman when you're shy, you will surely have a chapter that explains how to approach a woman, then a second on how to propose a date, then a third on how to behave during this date, before arriving at the chapter on how to conclude with a woman. It's a matter of logic, common sense.

You will not start your book by cutting corners and it seems logical to first approach a woman before thinking to conclude with her.

3rd Approach: Table of contents by needs.

This last approach no more consists in thinking in logical terms but in terms of needs.

You can try to identify the different needs around your subject, by listing the most frequently asked questions people have about the topic you deal with in your book. Each question you identify may be the subject of a chapter.

For example, if you make a book on how to get out of debt, you will find questions related to many cases of overindebted people (singles, couples, divorced, disabled etc.), and questions related to many ways to get out of that situation (how to find additional work, how to fill out an aid file, how to effectively approach a bank for a loan etc.). Each of these questions can be a different chapter.

Once you have listed all these questions and if your subject allows it, then I advise you to use the second approach to rearrange this list of questions into a logical table of contents where every question brings the reader a step closer to the final solution.

To identify the needs and questions people have on your subject, you can go for example to different forums related to your subject and see the different conversations between users.

An excellent general forum is Yahoo Answers (https://answers.yahoo.com/). Its main strength is that its high volume of daily visits can give a realistic representation of the most frequently asked questions.

Another good way is to look for popular blogs related to your topic and sign up for their newsletters to see the different questions they are answering. If the blog is popular, there's a good chance it has many daily visitors and that the blog posts provide a good representation of the kind of information people are trying to get.

Another way about which very few people think is to go to Amazon and use the "look inside" feature to look at the table of contents of competing books on the same topic that are in the best sales.

You should know that Amazon is by far one of the most visited site. So if a book ranks in the best sellers, there is a lot to bet that it answers important questions people have.

There are many other ways to find the most frequent questions people have about your topic, such as magazines in bookstores or ezines (electronic magazines).

Now, create your table of contents using one of the three approaches described above, and mix them if necessary.

Do not worry if your titles are badly formulated, we will optimize them during the sixth step. What matters the most for the moment is to create your plan in order to know what content you are going to put.

Once you have created your table of contents, you can move to the next step.

III.2.d- STEP 2: Create and annotate your structure.

Now you have your table of contents, you are going to create the structure of your book and annotate it.

Open your word processor and create a new document.

Write each title and subtitle of your table of contents at the top of a blank page, so that your entire table of contents is contained inside your document. Now, you only have one title or one subtitle written at the top of each blank page.

On each of the blank pages and thus for each title or subtitle, list all the points and ideas that you want to address.

At this point, simply use your existing knowledge on the subject and your experience to list these points and ideas.

It is not necessary to make sentences, you just need to list your ideas in order to know what you are going to write for each title and subtitle.

III.2.e- STEP 3: Complete your structure by an external search.

You may not have all the answers to the different titles and subtitles of your book. You have already written a maximum of your ideas using your knowledge, but you may find it seems incomplete and that some things are missing.

That's why you will now search information externally.

So take your structure and rescan each title and subtitle to add the points that can be more developed.

For each title and subtitle, make more precise searches with Google or with the resources we have seen previously when creating your table of contents (forums, targeted blogs, competing books on Amazon etc.).

You should be able to find the missing content and complete your list of points and ideas for each title and subtitle.

Once all this work is done and the architecture of your book is complete and balanced, your book now looks like a large list of points and ideas, structured as chapters thanks to your titles and subtitles.

Now, you only need to turn these points and ideas into sentences to give your content a readable form.

This is what we are going to see in the next step.

III.2.f- STEP 4: Turn the key points and ideas of your chapters into sentences.

Take your book from the beginning and write for each chapter a first version by developing the key points and ideas that are listed on it.

Write quickly, just as if you were talking to someone in front of you.

Use short sentences and simple words and go to the essentials.

Remember that you are not here to write a novel but to propose a solution to a problem your customers face.

So don't try to make poetry, this is not what your customers are looking for and it may even degrade the readability of your content that should remain simple and easy to understand.

Once you start writing a chapter, don't stop rereading or analyzing every sentence you write.

Follow word for word the quote of the famous writer Ernest Hemingway who said:

"Write drunk, edit sober."

This means that once you start writing, you must unleash your spontaneity and especially not stop to analyze and correct each of your sentences.

Perhaps you already know that the brain has two hemispheres, one creative and one analytical.

Stopping at the end of a sentence to make correction will instantly stop your creative brain inertia and activate your analytical brain instead.

Then as soon as you move to the next sentence, you must again stop your analytical brain to restart your creative brain.

Not only will this make you lose a lot of time, but your mind will also get tired a lot quicker.

So write without stopping, and don't worry about mistakes or bad turned phrases that you leave behind. You will have all the necessary time to correct and edit them in the next step.

For now, the only goal is to turn your lists of points and ideas into text paragraphs in draft mode without worrying about editing.

Furthermore, if you notice while you are writing that you still need to add information you don't have on hand, simply insert a comment in color or italics so you can easily come back later, and continue to write.

Once your book is fully written in draft mode and that you've added all the information you wanted, you can go to the next step which is all about editing your book.

III.2.g- STEP 5: Edit and refine your text.

Now that your book is completed in draft mode, you will be able to use your analytical brain to edit and correct any errors, bad turned phrases and refine your content.

Take your book and reread it from the beginning, chapter by chapter.

For each chapter, correct all your spelling mistakes. Rephrase any badly crafted sentence. Replace the words that are used too often by using synonyms. Make sure your paragraphs are linked in a logical and spontaneous way.

Reread it several times and each time refine a little bit more each one of your chapters until you are fully satisfied and that everything is optimized. Each of your chapters should be read with no effort, as if your text was flowing naturally.

Do not forget to aerate your text by skipping lines between paragraphs to make the reading easier.

Also, use this editing step to add several concrete examples in order to illustrate your ideas.

Use examples from your experience, experience of famous people, quote a passage from a book or a movie that marked you.

In short, tell stories and give concrete cases because anecdotes are often the things that will remain in the memory of the reader and that will allow him to easily understand an idea.

III.2.h- STEP 6: Enhance your titles and subtitles.

Now that your book is entirely written, it's time to review the wording of the main title of your book, as well as the titles and subtitles of your table of contents.

Indeed, by adding and modifying the content in the previous step, your titles and subtitles may not completely match with this content.

So, you need to restore this matching and make sure that your titles and subtitles perfectly illustrate the content under them.

In addition, you must make sure exclusively for a marketing purpose, that the main title of your book and the titles and subtitles of your chapters are attractive to instantly grab the reader's attention.

Make them impactful to capture the reader's attention.

Put yourself in reader's place and ask yourself if a book titled that way would make you stop to open it.

If the answer is no, keep looking for a catchy title until you find one that really grabs your attention.

Remember that if your book title is weak, no one will open your book to get a chance to discover the quality content you have created.

One of the best copywriter Gary Bencivenga gives this formidable formula to write a title that grabs attention and creates interest:

Benefit + Curiosity = Interest

If your headline promises at least one benefit and creates curiosity, then it will generate interest for the reader and you will win the game.

As mentioned in the formula, the greater the benefit and the curiosity, the higher the reader's interest.

There are countless ways to get a winning title, so trust your imagination.

In general, titles that promise precise and numerical results are very appreciated.

For example: "How to go from twenty to zero cigarettes in seven days" or "the secret method to learn by heart a one page text in 2 minutes."

In addition to your book title, also try rewording the titles and subtitles on the same principle in order to keep the attention of the reader awake all throughout your book, as if he was watching a suspense movie.

Your book is now almost finalized. You just need to reread it one last time and have it read by others.

III.2.i- STEP 7: Reread your book and have it read by others.

Your book finished, it's time to reread it entirely to make sure everything flows and links correctly and naturally.

It is also highly recommended to have it read by a few other people. Indeed, when you have your nose to the grindstone, you may not see some mistakes and imperfections that will jump out to the eyes of those who discover your book for the first time.

Better to discover these mistakes now rather than later, when your customers will start to give their negative feedback on the imperfections they see.

If you decide to have your book read by a few people before you officially publish it, choose people who belong to the audience targeted by your book. Tell these people that their opinion is important for you since they belong exactly to the audience you are targeting with your book.

If your book targets computer experts, you are not going to ask someone who barely knows how to use a computer to read your book.

The same way, if your book is addressed for men only, you are not going to ask women to read it.

Or if your book targets a young audience, you will not try to find reviewers among retired people.

On the contrary, if your book is intended for beginners in a particular field, look for people who have little or no knowledge in that field.

For example, if your book is a method to learn how to quickly play the guitar, ask people who do not know how to play the guitar to read your book.

Ask each of your readers what they did not understand, what could be improved, if other missing topics should be covered or if some points should be explained differently, and make corrections if necessary.

Once your book is finished, you just need to convert it into a digital format such as PDF (the most common), ePub or mobi.

III.3- How To Create A Video Product.

It is much easier to create a video product than a book, because you will not need to spend all that time writing.

Moreover, a video product usually has a higher perceived value compared to a book, so you could definitely sell it at a higher price.

This is what you are going to discover in the following pages.

III.3.a- Build your plan and choose the number of modules.

To start, you just need to build the plan of your video product and create one module for each chapter, with a number of modules generally ranging from three to seven video modules.

Indeed, some marketers believe that beyond seven modules, it is easy to lose the thread of the solution provided because it becomes harder for customers to have a global vision.

Let's say that four modules lasting 10 to 25 minutes each for a total of one hour is a good basis for your video product.

An acceptable range for a video product is between forty-five minutes and two hours.

Of course, the duration of each module and the number of modules will greatly depend on your topic and is given here as an indication of what is seen the most frequently in terms of standards.

You may for sure make a high quality video product such as a "Method to regain control of your time in 30 days" with thirty modules of two minutes each, where each module corresponds to one day.

Again, it will depend on the relevance and effectiveness of your content to solve your customers' problem.

It's much better to have a video product that lasts forty-five minutes and brings the perfect solution rather than a product which lasts three hours but missing the point completely and boring as hell.

Once your main plan is ready and that you have determined the number of modules of your video product, annotate for each module the points and ideas that you will address.

The idea here is just to list these points for each module but in no case should you write a script.

Indeed, these points will serve you as reminders when you will start the recording, but you do not need to recite any text, and you should absolutely avoid giving the impression that you are reading a script.

III.3.b- Attitude in front of the camera.

You have to know that to create a video product, you don't absolutely need to appear and show your head on the camera.

But if you decide to appear on the camera, there are some things to know about the attitude and the behavior to have in front of it.

Your approach in front of the camera should be natural and you'll certainly don't want to give the impression of reciting a text or reading a script, as seen previously.

You will have to speak and behave exactly as you do every day, as if you were explaining your topic to one of your friends.

It is proven that people listen more those who dress like them and talk like them.

So don't try to wear a $4000 tailored suit and tie and talk in a very complex and sophisticated language unless your product targets a very specific niche of professionals.

Remember that most of the time your customers will consume your video product from their home wearing casual clothes and with the familiar language they use at home and not at work.

So, show them you are like them when they look at you and just be yourself, with the clothes and the language you use when you are at home.

This way, your customers will appreciate you more, and you will also feel much more comfortable in front of the camera because your words will come in a natural way.

III.3.c- Record your video.

Before starting to record your different modules, repeat what you plan to say two or three times in front of your webcam. Watch the result and start again as many times you need to feel comfortable.

To create your video you can either do it yourself or call a professional.

If you do it by yourself, you can either choose to film yourself talking, or to make a screencast.

A screencast consists in filming your computer screen and in talking at the same time into the microphone to explain what you do.

This is very convenient especially if you make a training on how to use a particular software. You can make a complete training using a screencast, without ever having to show your face on camera.

Moreover, it is very quick to make a screencast and you can easily create a series of video training products within a week.

One of the best and most famous screencast softwares is certainly Camtasia Studio (available in Mac and PC version).

If instead of a screencast you decide to film yourself, you do not need to invest in the same equipment the greatest filmmakers have, since your goal is not to make movies like Spielberg.

The camera quality is much less important than the sound quality. So you just have to find at home a white wall or a neutral background, and put yourself in front of a camera put on a tripod.

If you do not have a lot of money, the webcam of your computer or the camera of your mobile phone can do the job.

For the sound, the microphone should be as close as possible to your mouth to ensure the best possible sound quality, because it is through the sound that your message will be delivered.

There is nothing worse than trying to understand what someone is saying because he is too far away or there is surrounding noise to hear him clearly.

Feel free to use an external microphone if necessary.

Once your recording equipment is installed, simply activate the camera and let it run.

If you miss a sequence or start confusing your ideas (which is very likely to happen especially if you are starting in video), do not panic. Simply start again at the beginning of that sequence.

Do not forget to leave a silence of 5 to 10 seconds between each module so that you could crop the files more easily during the editing.

These periods of silence will appear in your editing software and it will be easier to find out where to cut your video.

To be sure not to lose your plan, you have several ways.

The first is to have your notes next to you and to watch them discreetly whenever you need, like some journalists do.

You can also write your various talking points on a support in front of you that will not be visible on the video.

This support can be for example a board on which you write your different points, or a screen on which you project a PowerPoint presentation. You will be able to change the slides by a small remote control or by a colleague who will do it for you.

In case you want to be filmed but you do not want to do it by yourself, you can ask a professional.

The first quotations generally start at around $300. So, contact several companies to see the best deals. Given the simplicity of the video you want to make, you do not necessarily need a professional of great renown.

Just tell them you want to be filmed in front of the camera with a simple white or neutral background, and that the entire video will not last more than three hours.

III.3.d- Edit and package your video.

The video editing can easily be done by yourself.

Simply load your recording in a video editing software to remove the failed sequences and cut your recording in as many modules as needed.

As for the screencast, one of the best tools for video editing is certainly Camtasia Studio, but you can absolutely use softwares like Windows Movie Maker or iMovie if you are on Mac.

All these programs are very intuitive and easy to handle even if it is the first time you use them.

You can then save each of your modules in the MPEG4 (.mp4) format, which is the most common extension for video.

Finally, to package your video product, you can compress all of your modules into a single zip file using for example the compression software Winzip.

So, your video product is now contained in a single zip file, ready to be sold.

III.4- How To Create An Audio Product.

An audio product is perhaps what is the simplest and fastest to create compared to an ebook or a video product.

Here, you have no need to write nor need to be on camera and pay attention to your body language.

Like for a video product, start by building your plan and determine the number of modules of your audio product. The principles on the duration and number of modules are the same as for a video product.

Once your plan is built and you have listed for each module the points and ideas you are going to address, you are ready to start recording.

To record your audio product, you don't need some complicated devices. A simple portable recording device or the recorder of your phone will just do fine. Just make sure to speak close to the microphone to get an audible sound and of the best possible quality.

Before starting to recording your official version, you can make a few recordings to adjust your voice, your speech rate and remove hesitations.

If you find out there are some spluttering problems that can alter the sound quality, you can get a microphone windscreen or an anti pop filter.

Once you are ready to record the official version, activate your recorder and start talking.

If you make confusions with the ideas or forget to say something, repeat the sequence without stopping the recorder. You will cut the bad sequence during editing.

The same way as for a video product, leave five to ten seconds every time you start a new module, which will make your editing work much easier. Indeed, these silences will help you quickly determine where to cut your file to create the different modules.

Once everything is recorded, you can edit your audio file using a software like Audacity (free) or Camtasia Studio.

Simply remove the failed sequences and cut your file in as many modules as needed.

You can export each audio module in mp3, which is the most common format.

Finally, once all your modules are ready and in mp3, you can package them by gathering them in a single zip file that will be your final audio product ready to be marketed.

III.5- How To Create A Web App.

Web applications or "web apps" are programs that can only be executed on your Internet browser.

They offer all forms of online services, which can generally be used after paying a monthly subscription.

Among the many web apps that exist, you can for example find applications to organize your agenda, make a collaborative brainstorming session with several remote colleagues, perform a mind mapping, convert one file into another format, create invoices etc.

Examples of sites offering web apps:

Bubbl.us (https://bubbl.us/)
Online-Convert (http://www.online-convert.com)
Dropbox (https://www.dropbox.com/)

To make a web app, you can either do it by yourself if you have programming experience in JavaScript, or through a professional developer who will code it for you according to your specifications.

If you want to make your web app by yourself, there is an interesting service from Google that allows you to do it, called Google Apps Script: (http://script.google.com).

You can also find good developers at affordable prices, especially in places such as Elance (www.elance.com).

The website Fiverr (www.fiverr.com) can also provide an excellent price / quality ratio and with a little search, you can find a developer who can create your web app for just a few dollars to tens of dollars.

Before you jump in the creation of a web app, study well your market to find out what kind of web app can be highly successful.

The key factors of success for a web app are definitely the design, ergonomics and the ease of use.

So take a maximum care of the design even if you need to hire a professional designer for that, and make sure your web app is fun to use and user friendly.

Moreover, make it as intuitive as possible with simple actions and avoid at all costs complexity. People should never have to think : "how the hell does all this work?"

Finally, think about your pricing strategy as early as when you start the conception, for example by offering various deals that will give access to more or fewer features. You can also offer a free basic version that will capture the interest of your future customers and allow them to become familiar with the interface.

III.6- How To Create An Online Training.

You can create an online training and deliver it in a monthly subscription website with a members area.

Two of the best tools to build a membership site with a secure members area are Optimize Press (www.optimizepress.com) and Amember (www.amember.com).

The online training that you are going to create for the members of your website can use a variety of media, such as video, audio and text. Customers generally like to have a diversity of media.

The benefit of a monthly subscription website is that you really need to sell that once, and the rest of your income is recurring.

That's why a membership site is the golden way to really build an online financial empire because it allows you to increase your average shopping cart (the total amount of money a customer spends over months).

Then the goal will be primarily to maximize your retention rate and to try to find the right formula to keep your members as long as possible.

For this, you will need for instance to regularly offer new trainings and new tools at fixed times, to create a forum in your members area in which you answer all the questions asked by your subscribers that are related to your topic, to organize various events to meet your customers in the real life or during webinars, etc.

All the techniques are good, as long as they allow you to keep your subscribers as long as possible.

A good strategy to encourage your visitors to subscribe to your site is to offer the first month at a very low price and then a monthly debit at the normal price each following month.

For example, you can test and offer the first month at 1 dollar, then an automatic debit of $97 per month starting from the second month.

This engagement strategy is much more effective than directly offering a full price subscription right on the first month.

In fact, it completely eliminates the entry barrier that can prevent people from trying your online training formula.

III.7- Other Types Of Digital Products.

In addition to the products we have just discussed, there are a multitude of other digital products you can create.

For example, this can be a software application for mobile phone, a plugin for Wordpress etc.

This can also be in the form of services, for example by offering shopkeepers to set up their online store so they can be visible on the Internet.

You can also create your own online store. One of the best e-commerce software to create an online shop with a professional look is PrestaShop (https://www.prestashop.com). In addition, this e-commerce software is free and your online store can be installed in minutes.

If you do not have products to sell, you can fill your store with affiliate products that will make you earn a commission on every sale.

For example, Amazon has an affiliate program and even offers a free online store aStore (http://astore.amazon.com/). You can fill your store with all the Amazon products you want to sell, and the shop can be easily integrated into an existing website.

Think also about the opportunity to provide services that bring new prospects to professionals (lawyers, restaurants, plumbers, electricians etc.). There are a multitude of ways to be a business contributor.

For example, you can have a website that offers to make appointments with a notary or a lawyer in exchange of a commission.

Your site may well entice the visitor to call a number that will automatically redirect to the office of the notary or the lawyer with whom you are partnering.

Before being put in touch with the client, the notary or the lawyer will hear a message like: "This client is brought to you by Company X.".

III.8- Put Your Product On Paper Or CD/DVD Format.

This step is optional, and is for you if you want to put your ebook on a paper format or your other digital products on CD or DVD.

III.8.a- Advantages and disadvantages of a physical medium.

Before you decide to put your digital product on a physical medium, think about the advantages and disadvantages of both solutions.

On one hand, the physical medium can give your product more visibility, making it present for example on online retail stores that do not deal with digital products or that also deal with physical products like Amazon.

You also offer more visibility to your product that can be found on the shelves of some stores, making you free publicity and allowing you to take advantage of the associated sales.

The physical medium can also be perceived to have greater value as a digital product in some cases, for example in the case of a video product. A video is often more expensive when sold in a DVD format than in the form of a downloadable product.

That being said, this is generally not the case for books. A digital book sells generally two to three times more than a paper book.

Moreover, the physical medium will force you to consider logistical aspects that do not exist with the digital products, which can make your working process and your management more complicated.

III.8.b- How to put your product on a physical medium.

If you do not have budget or only a very limited budget, you can start by creating products on demand.

You can do this using the Amazon Createspace service (https://www.createspace.com) that allows you to create DVDs or paper versions of your products.

You can also use the Lulu Service (https://www.lulu.com/) to turn your digital book into a paper format.

Of course, by creating products on demand, they will cost slightly more than if you directly order them in large quantities.

That's why once you get your first customers, you can reinvest the profits to manufacture your products in larger quantities.

III.8.c- How to manage your logistics.

Once your digital product has been put on physical media, time is to see how to handle logistics.

Preparing and sending orders every day can quickly become time-consuming and tedious. This is why I highly suggest you to outsource logistics.

It will give you more time to develop your business and finally, outsourcing the logistics won't necessarily cost you more than if you do it all by yourself, since you would need to buy the envelopes, stamps at the post office, etc.

To outsource your logistics, you can use for example the excellent Amazon service called Fulfillment by Amazon (https://services.amazon.com/fulfillment-by-amazon/benefits.htm).

Simply send your products to an Amazon distribution center, and Amazon manages the storage, the packaging and the shipping, but also the customer service and the returns.

There are many other services that you can easily find if you search on the Internet.

This ends the part dedicated to the creation of your product. Whether your product is in digital or physical form, we will mainly talk about information products in the following pages.

That said, all of the techniques you are going to discover are easily adaptable to all other types of products.

IV- CREATE YOUR SALES PAGE (7 DAYS).

Your sales page is the place where you offer your product and where you make it available for purchase.

This is actually your sales pitch and it's the cornerstone of your marketing.

It's on this page that all the visitors who click on your ads will be sent.

Depending on how your sales page is built, it will convert more or less visitors into customers.

So it's in your best interest to have an effective sales page in order to get the highest possible conversion rate (in other words, the highest percentage of people who buy your product after reading your sales page).

The structure of a good sales page contains these seven elements:

- A shock title that captures attention.

- The problem and the false solutions of your customers.

- A photo that makes your product attractive.

- A list of customer benefits.

- The price presentation.

- Strong proofs.

- A call to action.

In the following pages, we are going to review these seven elements, and then see how to optimize more globally your sales page to make it as effective as possible right from its creation, in a design point of view, with the ergonomics, or with the best tone and style to adopt when writing your sales page.

And finally, we will see how to test your sales page to constantly improve its conversion rate, then we will end with the various ways of payment you can incorporate into your page.

IV.1- A Shock Title That Captures Attention.

The title is by far the most important thing of all your sales page.

So you need to choose it very carefully because you have no room for error.

Without a good title, you are assured that all the rest of your sales page will not be read, because you won't have managed to catch the reader's attention.

So, all the challenge is to find a shocking title that captures your reader's attention.

For this, there is the magic formula of Gary Bencivenga we have already seen in the III.2.g.

Remember, his formula says that to have a title that grabs attention and creates interest, it must both have a strong benefit and generate curiosity.

This formula can be summed up as this:

Benefit + Curiosity = Interest

The greater the benefit your product will bring to the customer, the higher the interest will grow in his eyes.

In other words, try to create a headline that promises to give the solution to the greatest desire or the greatest problem of your customer.

Here are some examples of strong benefits:

"Never again will you touch another cigarette!"
"Learning Spanish has never been so easy."
"Your diabetes problems stop here."

The same way, the more curiosity will be generated by your title, the more interest the customer will have for your product.

It is very effective here to use something that seems impossible and thus that will appear as shocking.

A good way is to use very precise and extreme metrics (time, distance, temperature, etc.), or to write something stupid or irrational.

The idea is always the same: the more you will intrigue the reader by making him wonder "how the hell could that be possible?", the more he will want to continue reading.

By adding the curiosity element to the previous examples, the title really becomes irresistible:

"Never again will you touch another cigarette! The proven method to stop smoking in less than 45 minutes and without patch."

"How to stop smoking before tonight by peeling a potato."

"Learning Spanish has never been so easy. Go to Spain next week being bilingual."

"Your diabetes problems stop here. Here is how this countryside doctor gets 100% of cured patients with this surprising remedy."

As you can see in the examples above, it is also possible to write the title in two sentences.

The first sentence can be used to capture attention, and the second sentence can be a subtitle that shows the main benefit, specifies or adds a note of curiosity.

To sum up: Bring in your headline a strong benefit and a high curiosity, and you will the game.

You can train yourself and get inspired by looking at the book or magazine titles that grab your attention or that are best sellers.

IV.2- The Problem And The False Solutions Of Your Customers.

Once you've found a catchy title, you can (if you want) quickly reformulate the promise of your title with one or two introductory phrases (eg, "In the following lines, you're going to discover how to ...").

Then, it's time to detail the problems and false solutions of your customers.

For example :

"Are you tired of ...?"
"You can not stand anymore to..."
"You don't manage to... and feel like you're in a dead end?"

Insist on the problems and don't hesitate to dramatize the situation in order to make your customers aware that this is really something annoying and that they must absolutely find a solution.

Then start to mention the false solutions, and all they have already tried to solve the problem:

"Perhaps you've already tried to X or Y ... but ..."

Show them here that the solutions which most people who have the same problem think about don't work.

For example for tobacco:

"You may unsuccessfully have already tried patches or electronic cigarettes but you still can not resist the urge to smoke a real one."

They must understand that the solution you propose them is something unique and different from all the rest.

IV.3- A Photo That Makes Your Product Attractive.

People are very sensitive to have a visual representation of the product they are about to buy because they usually need to see exactly what they are buying.

Imagine a salesman who tries to sell you a pair of shoes without showing them to you. Rather difficult, isn't it?

Now imagine that you see a pair of shoes in a store window. You are almost immediately able to say whether or not you want the pair.

So do not neglect the photo of your product, because if it's ugly or does not arouse a desire to purchase the product, they are not going to want to buy it and you will lose sales.

Do not hesitate to put everything into it to get a photo that makes your product extremely desirable.

If you are not sure about your talents to make great photos, go and see a professional photographer.

If your product is virtual (such as an ebook), you can easily create a 3D image with a software such as Quick3Dcover, simply by having the 2D book cover image.

You can easily find this software by doing a simple Google search, and there are also many other softwares that do exactly the same thing.

You can also use one or more photos of people currently using the product, or experimenting the benefits of the product.

It is possible to find many royalty-free photos for a few dollars on Fotolia (www.fotolia.com), iStockphoto (www.istockphoto.com) or Shutterstock (www.shutterstock.com).

If you want royalty-free photos without spending a dime, you can find some on Freerangestock (http://freerangestock.com/index.php), StockVault (http://www.stockvault.net/), or EveryStockPhoto (http: / /www.everystockphoto.com/).

In these cases, read carefully the conditions of use of the images. In some cases, you will be asked to add a link to the license, or the name of the photographer next to the photo.

If you search well in these huge stocks of photos, you will surely find exactly what you need.

However, I strongly recommend you to absolutely avoid pictures that look like clichés or that sound completely fake (you will find many pictures of that kind in these image bank websites).

For example, do not choose businessmen shaking hands and dressed with a beautiful costume right in the middle of the World Trade Center.

Do not choose a stunning blonde girl happy to type on a computer and smiling with teeth whiter than snow.

Choose pictures that convey emotion and that does not sound fake. Your business depends on it.

IV.4- A List Of Customers Benefits.

It is much more important for a customer to know the benefits of a product than its characteristics.

For example, it is much more important for a customer who buys a washing machine to know that he is buying a way to wash clothes rather than simply saying that he is buying a "washing machine".

The same way, when you buy a Bluetooth microphone, you do not buy a microphone but a way to walk and move easily without being annoyed by a wire.

It's not the product in itself that interests you, but the result you will get by using that product.

This is why you should always first try to list a maximum of benefits of your product, and then use the characteristics of your product to prove that each benefit listed is true and real.

The traditional method consists in first mentioning the customer benefit and then listing just below the characteristic(s) that allow to obtain this benefit.

Here are some examples :

- "Computer equipped with an HDMI output" becomes: Watch your favorite movies directly on your TV: the computer is equipped with an HDMI output.

- "Store open 7 days / 7" becomes:

You can even do your shopping on Sunday: the store is open 7 days / 7.

- "64 GB memory card included" becomes:
Make extra long videos immediately: a 64 GB memory card is included with the product.

- "Advanced color management panel" becomes:
Get professional quality videos in one click thanks to an advanced color management panel.

You see the huge difference it creates?

IV.5- The Price Presentation.

The goal here is to create the impression that the price of your product is ridiculously low compared to all it would cost the customer if he doesn't decide to use your product.

You have to make it crystal clear for the customer that he will get a R.O.I (Return On Investment) at least five times equal to the price he is going to pay to purchase your product.

This return on investment can be monetary, but it can also be temporal, medical or of any other kind.

What matters is to allow the customer to see the return on investment translated into dollars.

For example, if your product is a solution to stop smoking, there will be a clear financial return on investment, which is to completely stop buying packets of cigarettes.

If your product costs 97 dollars, a smoker who consumes a packet per day and pays 6.5 dollars for each packet, he will have saved five times the price of your product in less than three months.

In addition, there will also be a return on investment related to your health, making you potentially saving thousands of dollars in surgery in case of clogged arteries.

If your product is a fast reading method, try to estimate the loss of money that the customer may face if he remains a slow reader (missing critical information everyday that can cost him hundreds or thousands of dollars).

You can also estimate the savings the customer will make compared to other existing solutions.

For example if your product costs 47 dollars and allows people to lose 45 pounds in a month, compare that price to the cost of one year special dietary program menus that would allow to lose exactly the same weight.

HOW TO SET YOUR PRODUCT PRICE.

Finding the right price is relatively complicated and will require you to perform many tests.

I advise you to offer an introductory price, then do several promotions and see what works best for your product.

In general, you must display the same price for all your customers and you do not have the right to have different prices for the same product at the same time.

You have however the right to make promotions, as long as they show a deadline and are the same for all your visitors.

To set your price, you will have to know the perceived value your customer has about your product.

The more perceived value your product will have, the higher you could price it, regardless of how much it cost you to manufacture it and regardless of the prices of your competitors.

Indeed, the customer does not care at all about your manufacturing costs.

Whether the product cost you a lot or almost nothing to produce is not important. In all cases, if your product does not solve his problem, he will not pay to get it.

This is why the more important is the problem solved by your product, the more the customer will be ready to pay a high price because the product will represent a lot of value for him.

This is how you can set higher prices than the competition without any problem.

Here is an example to understand the concept of perceived value of your product.

Imagine you sell a bottle of water of 16.9 fl. oz in the heart of New York.

You can hope to sell it for one or two dollars, but not much more because you do not solve a problem. At worst, the customer had a sudden small thirst and decided on impulse to buy your bottle.

Now imagine that you are selling the same bottle of water in the middle of the desert. This time, the bottle of water becomes vital for your customer and he sees its value as a potential lifesaver.

Thus, he will be ready to pay much more than a couple of dollars, maybe forty or fifty dollars for the same bottle.

This way, the more you will manage to make your product be perceived as having a high value, the more you could set high prices.

This is also why I advise you, if you sell an ebook or a DVD, to avoid using a vocabulary that focuses on the container and to use instead a vocabulary that focuses on the content.

For that, just replace the words related to the container such as "ebook" or "DVD" with words related to the content such as "method" or "system".

Again, finding the right price is a matter of testing.

Test the same price by changing your sales pitch and test several prices for each pitch to find the formula that works best.

IV.6- Strong Proofs.

The golden rule for a successful sales pitch is to systematically add a proof right after any claim saying that your product is the best.

You can use two types of proofs: the social proof and the authority proof.

Social proof draws its strength from the number of other people who are already customers.

Its goal is to deliver the following message:
"So many people are customers, why not me?"

Here are some examples of social proof:

"The preferred product of the 25-35 years old."

"Already 7,000 customers."

"US best seller."

The authority proof draws its strength using advices from experts.

The message to be delivered is:
"This product is recommended by experts, I trust them."

Some examples:

"Recommended by the scientific X, expert in such field."

"84% of specialists use the product X."

"Seen on TV."

"The most used product among pilots."

If you can, use both types of proofs. It will only enhance the strength of your pitch and its capacity to convince.

HOW TO EASILY GET CUSTOMERS TESTIMONIALS.

Getting real customers testimonials is essential to every effective sales page.

Here is a method that works like crazy, and that will allow you to get customers testimonials without any effort or additional time.

In addition, these testimonials will be real and not invented (a practice that is totally illegal).

The idea is to create a customer satisfaction questionnaire, and send it to your clients after seven days or more after their purchase.

You can automate the sending of this questionnaire using an autoresponder such as Aweber (www.aweber.com), Getresponse (www.getresponse.com) or Icontact (www.icontact.com).

You simply need to write an email in which you put the link to your satisfaction questionnaire, and the service will to send it for you at the desired time after the purchase.

This way you are assured that all your customers will receive the satisfaction questionnaire at the same time, and that you will not have forgotten anyone.

To create the questionnaire, you can use free services such as Google Docs (www.google.com/docs) that will automatically gather all the responses in an Excel file, or a dedicated service such as Survey Monkey (www.surveymonkey.com).

Write questions in a way that the customers answers will create a positive testimonial you could then use to serve the cause of your product.

For example :

"How product X helped you solve that problem?"

"What aspect of product X do you like more than its competitors?"

At the end of the questionnaire, add a check box allowing you to publish the answers, for example:

"I authorize X to publish my answers."

Most people will allow you to publish their answers.

This method is one of the most effective to obtain relevant testimonials in a completely legal way.

You can of course use this questionnaire to identify things to improve or to add to your product.

IV.7- A Call To Action.

Did you know that it is possible to increase from 10 to 15% the number of sales just by changing the text on and around the link to the payment page?

The goal here is to clearly indicate the action the customer must do.

It may seem weird or stupid, but people need to be told exactly what to do.

For example :
"Click here to receive your training."

To have a strong and effective call to action, I suggest you use elements that bring urgency in terms of limited time or limited quantities, to urge the customer to buy and prevent him from postponing his decision.

Some examples :

"Buy now: click here to order."

"Get your training now."

"Offer valid only 24h: order now."

"Offer valid while stocks last."

"Only 14 copies remaining: get yours immediately."

"Limited stocks: click here for instant purchase."

Another technique is to mention again the biggest benefit of your product on the text just above or immediately below the link to the payment page.

For example :

"Become a master of Spanish in one weekend. Get the method now:"

"Make professional videos with one click. Start now:"

Last thing, double as much as possible the buying links, with a button and a text link.

For some reason, some people prefer to order by clicking on a button and others on a text link.

For example, put on the button something like:
"Buy immediately"

And on the text link below:
"Click here to order now"

You have a wide choice of possibilities to improve your call to action.

Get inspired also with the other famous and successful online shopping sites to see how they make their call to action.

We'll see in the next section how to optimize your entire sales page, including the design of your purchase buttons that plays a critical role in the effectiveness of the call to action.

IV.8- Optimize Your Sales Page.

The only purpose of your sales page is to sell your product, and you will remove and change here all the things that do not serve this single purpose.

Start by removing all unnecessary links that lead to things other than the payment page. You do not want your visitors to spread. You want to keep them focused and to stay on the sales page, and not leave the page by clicking here and there.

The only action that the client must be able to do is to click the buy button.

So delete the menu and links that lead to other pages of your website.

The same way, delete all advertisements, banners and affiliate links that might be on your sales page.

Eventually, you can just keep a link to the terms and conditions at the very bottom of your sales page, another for the legal notices and one for the contact form. But that's all.

The visitor should also instantly see what your page is about and see a first purchase button at the very top of your sales page and above the fold (in other words before he could scroll down your page using the scroll bar on the screen side).

For the general design, minimalism is also the best option. Avoid bulky designs and opt for a simple and clean design.

The design of each of your sales buttons is also crucial. Make your buy button large and very visible, even playful. This is what works best.

If you do not know how to make a great and efficient buy button, you can create one for free in just a few mouse clicks using a site such as Da Button Factory (http://dabuttonfactory.com/) or Button Optimizer (http://buttonoptimizer.com).

Put selling buttons regularly throughout your sales page. Feel free to insert buy buttons among any long list of benefits or promises you may have in your sales page.

Analyze the places of your sales page where visitors put their mouse cursor and place the purchase buttons at these locations. To identify these zones, you can use a heatmap with services such as Crazy Egg (www.crazyegg.com).

In addition, each of these purchase buttons should lead as soon as possible on the payment page. The best is that right after a customer clicks on the buy button, he is redirected to the online payment page where he will be able to enter his credit card details.

So avoid to the maximum to get the customer who clicks on the buy button into many extra steps before allowing him to make his payment (account creation, email address verification, filling many unnecessary fields etc.).

It will just create more frustration and make you lose sales.

Eventually, it will be time to do all these secondary steps once the payment has been completed.

Now we are going to see in the following pages the style and tone to adopt to write your sales page.

IV.9- The Style And Tone Of Your Sales Page.

If you apply these few simple writing rules, you will increase your sales by 30% without needing to have more traffic and without changing your price.

USE SHORT SENTENCES.

First, use short sentences.

The rule is to have one information per sentence. If you have two, cut the sentence and create two sentences instead.

USE SIMPLE WORDS.

No need to use complex words to appear serious and talk about "synchronization by boolean semaphores of the parallel processes of image treatment optimization" to promote a photo editing software.

You are not here to spread your knowledge and show how smart you are but to sell. The client will perhaps find that you seem serious (if ever he understands everything), but he may get bored so quickly that he may leave your page very fast because you will not have managed to simplify his reading.

Remember that the customer who reads your pitch shouln't have to make any understanding effort, or he will leave you.

So swallow your envy to show your science and use simple words that everyone easily understands.

AERATE.

Go to the next line as much as necessary. Skip lines more frequently than you usually do. Shorten your paragraphs.

Your text must breathe, so aerate-it.

USE THE BOLD AND / OR HIGHLIGHTING.

Most people do not read, they scan.

They quickly go through the sales page until they find a word or a part that grabs their attention, and on which they are going to stop and start reading in details.

Thus, the idea is that all your sales pitch should be fully understood simply by reading what is in bold.

TALK ABOUT THE CUSTOMER INSTEAD OF ABOUT YOU.

Your pitch shouldn't be focused on you but on the customer and his problem.

So use to the maximum the terms "you", "your", "your" instead of "I" or "we" and focus on your client.

The customer is much less interested in knowing how great and prestigious your company is than he is about solving his problems.

Have a look for example at these two radically different approaches:

1- Alpha Computing is a strong provider with 2,000 employees and recognized in over 50 countries for its excellence in configuration management.

2- Wherever you are in the world and at any time, your configuration management is fully taken care of: 2,000 employees dedicated to you 24h / 24 in over 50 countries at Alpha Computing.

Do you see the clear difference of point of view?

The second text is entirely focused on the client, while the first one is only focused on the company.

Talk about the customer and stop talking about you.

USE A JOURNALISTIC AND NOT A COMMERCIAL TONE.

Your page should not look like a commercial speech in which you make your self-promotion.

Instead, you must use a journalistic tone and bring information to your reader.

In the same way that a newspaper article do, you should provide quality content and teach something relevant to those who read it, about your product and what can be done with this product.

If you adopt an overly promotional style, it will tend to scare away your customers.

Here is an example of a promotional title:

"A revolutionary system to become the best chess player in the world."

The title clearly expresses a specific position and a lack of objectivity.

Instead, make it objective and informative, exactly as would do the newspapers and magazines:

"An innovative system to become an expert in chess."

"Becoming a chess champion in a week, is it really possible?"

So use an objective, journalistic style in your entire sales page, right from the main title until the last word.

IV.10- Use Split-Testing.

If you followed the previous advices, then you have already done the best you could do to have a good sales page.

But that is not enough. You'll have to constantly test this page, comparing it to a variant of this page to see which version works best.

This is called split testing. The idea is to distribute the visitors on different versions of your sales page.

I suggest you always test only two versions of your sales page at the same time (this is called A / B Testing). This way, you won't get confused by having too many parameters to analyze.

Similarly, only change one parameter at a time in your sales pages, otherwise you will not be able to identify the parameter responsible for a best conversion result.

Some examples of A / B tests:

Example 1:
Version A with a red button.
Version B with a yellow button.

Example 2:
Version A with a title 1.
Version B with a title 2.

Example 3:
Version A with an image of your product.
Version B with a different image of your product.

Etc.

For each test, select the page that gave the best conversion rates, and replace the losing version with a new one that will test another parameter.

Of course, you need to wait enough to get a representative number of transformations in order to designate without error the page that gave the best results.

This is also why I advise you to test only two different versions of your sales page at the same time, because if your traffic is low, you may wait for months before collecting enough significant results to make a decision.

Do this indefinitely to continually improve your sales pages, and always test two different versions simultaneously. Work on your test step by step, element by element.

Although split testing takes time, it is the most effective way to get a profitable sales page.

WHICH TOOL TO USE TO DO SPLIT TESTING.

One of the best tools to do split testing is free, it is Google Analytics (https://www.google.com/analytics/).

It is very simple to use. Just paste the code provided by Google Analytics at the top or at the bottom of the different versions of your sales pages.

Then, the tool will automatically send visitors to one or the other version.

The transformations are measured by a code that analyzes the number of visits to the confirmation page after purchase (for example the thank you page).

As I explained earlier, I advise you to only use the A / B Testing option of Google Analytics and not the tests with multiple variables.

IV.11- Methods Of Payment.

There are a multitude of choices to choose the payment method that suits you best.

Your bank also probably offers ways to manage your online payments.

You can also use Paypal (www.paypal.com), which is one of the most widely used and common payment methods.

In addition, it offers a daily payment, which allows you to accelerate the process of "buying advertising> selling> buying more advertising" and thus to quickly expand and scale-up your campaign, even if you started it with a tiny budget.

Here are some other payment systems:

Commerce Gate (www.commercegate.com)
Authorize.Net (www.authorize.net)
2Checkout (www.2checkout.com)

Anyway, you should pay attention to several criteria when choosing an online payment system.

Choose a payment system with ergonomic pages and that inspire trust.

According to the payment system you choose, the payment pages may have very variable designs and ergonomics that either inspire trust and confidence or on the contrary inspire distrust and sow doubt.

So be careful with that because poor ergonomics can make you lose customers by preventing people from buying.

Also, pay attention to how often you will be paid.

The quicker you will be paid, the quicker your could use the money to expand your campaigns. That's why, avoid choosing a payment system that pays you on a monthly basis.

Also look at the percentage of commission charged by the payment system for each transaction. The commission will often decrease according to the volume of monthly sales.

Finally, you should know that certain payment systems will also keep a small percentage (rolling reserve) of what you earn to protect themselves in case of customer complaints or refund claims (chargeback).

Thus, the more your business will face a high number of refund requests, the more you may have to pay your payment system provider, and the more the rolling reserve will be important.

V- PROMOTE YOUR SALES PAGE (7 DAYS).

Now that your sales page is ready, you need now to attract quality traffic, which is traffic that must simultaneously be fast, laser targeted and massive.

We are going to see in the following pages how to quickly get such quality traffic.

V.1- Launch Advertising Campaigns.

One of the most effective ways is to use an advertising network like Google Adwords (www.google.com/adwords).

This way, you will be able to display your ad in the ads spaces that Google makes available next to the organic search results when a user types a keyword related to your product.

Do not expect to see your sales page naturally appear in the Google organic search results when a user types a keyword related to your product. SEO usually takes months, and a simple sales page will not contain enough content to make Google rank it in the first results.

The only way to get a chance to be on the first page of Google (which is essential because over 90% of Internet users who search for something will not even see the second page according to a study lead by Chitika Insights) is to use their Adwords advertising network and to see your ads appear.

Adwords is based on the principle of cost per click (CPC). In other words, when someone types a keyword related to your product on Google, your ad will be displayed in the dedicated advertising space but you only pay if the user clicks on your ad. You do not pay the fact of displaying your ad.

The cost per click depends on several factors, including competition which is the most important. The more advertisers are competing on a keyword, and the more your cost per click will be high if you want to appear in a good position. This is an auction based system.

Another factor affecting your cost per click will be your click through rate (CTR), which is the ratio between the number of clicks on your ad compared to the number of times your ad is displayed.

For example, if 19 users click on your ad that appeared 100 times, your CTR will be 19%.

So, your goal will be to obtain the highest possible CTR for each one of your ads, which will allow you to pay less your cost per click.

Indeed, if your CTR is low, it means that Google uses its advertising space to display ads that are not clicked, and thus that don't bring it money. To compensate this, Google will increase the price of your cost per click. That's why you need to have a CTR as high as possible.

We will see in the following pages the strategy that I use to create my advertising campaigns for each new product launch.

V.1.a- Establish a list of very specific keywords.

The first most important step is to make a list of very specific keywords related to your product.

Your goal will be to find keywords that are highly searched by users and that have little competition and thus a lower cost per click.

For now, list precisely the keywords that you would spontaneously type in Google in order to see your ad appear.

Avoid keywords composed of only one word and try to find as much as possible keywords of several words. The more words your keywords will have, the lower competition you will face and the more precisely you will target the users who will click on your ad.

It is far better to have a long list of 100 keywords that each have 200 monthly searches rather than a single short keyword that has 20,000 monthly searches.

Indeed, not only the short keyword will face a lot of competition which will force you to pay a very expensive cost per click, but it will also bring you more untargeted traffic and visitors who have no interest in your product.

For example if you are selling Nike shoes that automatically lace up and ask Google to display your ads whenever someone types the word "shoes", you will be competing with all the other shoes sellers, no matter the brand or the characteristics.

If a woman is looking for high heels shoes and she simply types "shoes", your ad will appear.

And if your ad appears, she will see that it does not correspond to her search and there is a good chance that she will not click on your ad, which will lower your CTR and thus you will pay more your cost per click to Google.

And if ever she decides to click on your ad for some reason, she will not be interested in your Nike shoes and you will lose money.

However, if you sell these particular Nike shoes but choose a long keyword such as "Nike shoes that lace up by themselves", that keyword will be certainly less typed than the word "shoes" in the Google search bar, but you will attract users who are looking for exactly the product you are selling.

Not only will you have a lot less competition which will lower your cost per click, but there is also a strong chance they will click on your ad, which will increase your CTR and thus decrease your cost per click.

So make a list of keywords as specific as possible.

The next step is to measure the number of monthly searches and competition for each keyword you have just listed, and also to refine your keywords search by finding new ones, in order to select your winning keywords.

V.1.b- Refine your keywords search with Keyword Planner.

Once you have established your list of specific keywords, submit it to the free tool from Google (already seen in II.2.b), the Keyword Planner (https://adwords.google.com/KeywordPlanner).

This tool will give you the monthly search volume for each of your keywords, an indication of the competition and will suggest a cost per click that will ensure you to have your ad in a good position if someone types the corresponding keyword.

Moreover, you can target these indicators by country, region or language. For example, if your sales page is in English and you want to sell your product only in the US or in a city like Dallas, you don't need to select the rest of the world because you are not concerned by displaying your ad to people who live in Argentina, Germany or in the UK.

Also, remove from your list the keywords that have almost no traffic and where competition is too strong.

Use the additional keywords and synonyms the tool suggests you in order to find good alternatives to the keywords you have just removed.

As we mentioned above, the idea is to find keywords with little competition but with enough monthly searches.

For this you can take for example a basic keyword and refine the search by adding details to that keyword.

Let's say you want to sell laptop batteries, and you have the basic keyword "laptop batteries".

The Keyword Planner may suggest you expressions that complement that keyword, but you can also complete this keyword by adding for example a laptop brand such as "Dell laptop batteries", or a characteristic such as "long duration laptop batteries", or any other specificity, and see the resulting search volumes. This way, you will be able to refine and enrich your keywords list.

Finally, choose keywords that filter users who do not intend to buy your product but just intend to watch.

For example, if you are promoting a professional website about photography, many Internet users will visit the site only to watch the pictures and find inspiration, without any intention of buying anything.

You must absolutely avoid that kind of people to click on your ads.

For this, you must put yourself in the mind of a potential customer who is looking for you on Google, and see the keywords he might type to find you and that people who have no intention to buy would never type.

For example "professional photography prices" or "wedding picture quote". It is your mission to find these keywords according to your niche market.

Additional note:
If you already use the Keyword Planner tool (formerly Keyword Tool), you have to know that it now displays only

the monthly search volumes corresponding to the exact match of the keywords you enter. So you no longer need to put your keywords into brackets to avoid having the volumes of the broad match or the phrase match, as it was the case in the past.

V.1.c- Group your keywords per topic.

The next step consists in grouping your expressions by topics around an unique keyword.

The idea is to later link each of the created keywords groups to a different ad, adapted to these expressions.

Grouping the ads by topic will have the merit of increasing your CTR (click through rate) thanks to a better targeting.

For example :

Group 1:
Learn the guitar
Learn the guitar online
Learn the guitar on Internet
Learn the guitar in Chicago

Group 2:
Guitar lessons
Online guitar lessons
Guitar lessons on Internet
Guitar lessons in Chicago

Etc.

Create on your Adwords account a separate group of ads for each of your keywords lists (each campaign can be divided into multiple ad groups).

V.1.d- Write your ads.

Your campaign is almost ready and you only need to write your ads to finish it.

The goal is to write ads that will make people click, in order to increase the CTR (click through rate) and thus reduce your cost per click.

A good technique to write ads on which users will want to click is to include in the ad title the exact keyword searched by the user, or at least the main keyword of expression he used for his Google search.

This way, he will see that your ad contains the same keyword he typed, and he will be more inclined to click on your ad.

For example, if I search "learn the guitar" and I see a link that displays "learn the guitar", I would certainly be more inclined to click on this particular link than if I read "guitar lessons".

Moreover, if the keyword in your ad matches the one entered by the visitor, Google will display the keyword in bold in your ad, which will improve even more the click rate by making your ad more visible.

This is also one of the reasons why it is important to group your keywords by theme as explained above, in separate ad groups.

For each ad group, write two ads that will contain the main keyword in the title.

Then the aim will be to split test these ads (for example to show the first ad 50% of times when the keyword is typed and the second ad the remaining 50% of times), and see for each ad group which one of the two gives the best click rate.

And to repeat the experiment indefinitely in order to continuously improve the campaign.

V.1.e- Measure your results.

It is crucial to measure the results obtained by your ads in order to improve them.

Adwords allows you to measure it very simply, by providing detailed reports of all the metrics you need such as the transformation rate of ads groups, of each ad, of each keyword, as well as the cost per transformation (the price you have to pay in advertising to get one customer).

Delete the ineffective keywords and ads that do not convert visitors into customers, and allocate the corresponding budget to new keywords, new ads, or to existing keywords and ads that seem to convert more.

This way, you will gradually improve your cost per transformation by gradually increasing the margin between what you must pay in advertising costs to get a new customer and what you earn when a customer buys your product.

To access these data and view them on your account, you only need to allow Adwords to collect them by copying the code provided by Adwords and pasting it on the page that follows the purchase of your product (for example the thank you page of your website).

V.1.f- Start small, then increase your budget.

Start with a small budget by investing an amount you can afford to lose every day.

The purpose of the initial bet is to accumulate statistics to know what are the most profitable keywords and those that make you lose money.

Once you have reached twenty or thirty transformations, you will have enough statistical data to draw conclusions on the keywords that work and those that do not bring results.

You can then review your bets by focusing on keywords that work and removing those that make you lose money.

The same way, analyze the results of each one of the two ads you wrote. Keep the one that gave you the best results and replace the other with a new ad.

The idea is to always test two ads at the same time in each ads group to continuously improve the click through rate.

If your campaign is not profitable from the very beginning do not worry, this is completely normal.

It's only by continuously improving the selection and the bets on your keywords and ads that you will manage to get very promising results.

Once you determine the threshold at which you start making profits and that you know your earnings per dollar spent, it's time to increase your advertising budget by reinvesting what you are earning.

If for instance you know that your customers make you earn $1.48 for every dollar you spend on advertising, this means that you win $148 for $100 spent and $ 1,480 for $1,000 spent.

When this happens, it's time to scale everything up and invest the maximum amount of money as fast as you can in order to get a maximum of profits by reaching the traffic limits that Google can provide you.

When you manage to establish this kind of dynamic, your sales process works almost automatically and you create a real machine to generate cash.

This is all the advantage of having a payment system such as Paypal, which allows you to be paid on a daily basis and thus to be able to quickly reinvest the money you earn.

Imagine the problems you could have with a system that pays you only once a month and the time you would waste to bring your campaigns to maturity.

Note that in addition to Google Adwords, you can use other extremely interesting other pay per click platforms such a Bing Ads (http://advertise.bingads.microsoft.com/en-us/home) which captures more than 30% of the US online market and which is the second largest pay per click network in the world.

Also, you have Adknowledge
(http://www.adknowledge.com) which is the fourth largest
ad marketplace and which is landing page friendly.

You may also have very attractive costs per clicks on these
two alternative platforms.

V.2- Use The Content Network.

Google Adwords also gives you the opportunity to display your ads on its Display network of its partner sites (http://www.google.com/ads/displaynetwork/).

This is composed of all blogs, news sites and forums used by Google Adsense to generate income. Google then displays different ads or banners on a dedicated place of the blog or website, and you can display your ad like that.

However, be aware that the click and conversion rates are in general very low, but it can complete your Adwords campaigns if you manage to make your campaign on the Display Network effective enough to make more money than you spend.

If you choose to advertise on the Google Display Network partner sites, I recommend creating a separate campaign and dedicated to that purpose.

I also advise you to make a targeting by website and not by keyword.

For that, identify the websites and blogs in your topic on which it would be relevant to display an advertisement for your product.

You just have to select the option "Relevant pages only on the placements and audiences I manage" in the "Networks and devices" of your campaign settings.

Your ads will then automatically be displayed on the sites you select.

Over time, analyze the results of your ads for each of the chosen sites by consulting your Adwords statistics.

Remove your ads from sites that do not bring you anything, and raise your bids on those that give you good results.

Rather than text ads, what works best on the Display network are banners.

Avoid banners with too small sizes such as 125x125.

After several tests, the banners sizes of 300x250 or 468x60 are the ones that work best.

Regarding the design of your banners, what works best is not necessarily what is the most aesthetic or the most elaborate.

For example, you can create a document in the desired format on Photoshop or Gimp, paste your ad that works best and circle it with a red pen or place arrows around it.

Try adding as much as possible arrows and buttons on your banners, it improves the click through rate.

You can also incorporate a human image, in particular an image of woman since they tend to have a higher click rate than men.

Regarding animations on banners, Google tends to dislike them, in particular flashing banners, which are forbidden.

However, you can use moving elements, which can sometimes make you even double your click through rate.

If you do not want to create your banners yourself, you can use the excellent 20DollarBanners Service (http://www.20dollarbanners.com/) which makes professional banners and ensures you to get optimal click rates.

Once you have determined the sites on which you have the best click and conversion rate, you can directly contact these sites and negotiate with them a special price to display your advertisements without having to go through Google Adwords.

You can certainly find a good compromise where you're both winners: you get a price lower than the average cost per click you pay with Google, and in return they are paid more than if you go through Adwords since you no longer have to pay a commission to Google.

You can also negotiate a fixed monthly price, regardless of the number of clicks or displays of your ad. This solution can often be the cheapest for you.

V.3- The Case Of Facebook Ads : Profitable Or Not?

Nielsen Research estimates that less than 1% of online sales come from Facebook, and that the transformation rate into customers on Facebook is 0.07%, against 1% on a classic merchant site.

In other words, if your goal is to directly sell your product using Facebook Ads (https://www.facebook.com/advertising), forget about it right away.

And it makes sense.

Users go to Facebook to connect with their friends, have fun, play, but not to buy a product.

However, what works extremely well with Facebook advertising is asking users to do a simple action and that does not immediately demand a large commitment such as buying a product.

For example: to register on a mailing list in order to receive a free gift or a discount coupon.

Thus, the best strategy for a profitable campaign with Facebook Ads is to create a capture page that provides a valid reason to subscribe and then, to send a sequence of automated emails using autoresponder services such as Aweber (as discussed in the IV.6), in order to redirect the subscribers on your sales page and sell your product.

Sites offering daily discounts such as Groupon or AppSumo are good success examples with Facebook Ads.

Once you click on their ads, they just ask your email address. It's only later that they will start to sell you things, through the emails you will receive from them.

The advantage of Facebook compared to Adwords is that you can target users based on criteria as specific as the geographical location, gender, age, interests, places where the person worked, etc.

Regarding the cost per click, it is directly related to your click through rate (CTR).

Once you create your ad, Facebook will suggest a bid range.

When you start, simply choose a bid close to the lower end of this range.

Your CTR will then quickly begin to dictate the price you will pay for traffic:

If your CTR is high, the price of the suggested bids is going to decrease.

If your CTR is low, you will need to increase your bid for each click.

I suggest you start with a daily budget of just a few dollars. Less than 10 dollars are generally enough to make Facebook start suggesting you new ranges of bids with a much lower price.

Use them to reduce your bet and still remain close to the lower end of the bid range, and raise your daily budget.

Optimize continuously your ads and your targeting in order to permanently increase your CTR.

V.4- Build Your Resellers Network.

Would you be interested in having an army of people who sell your product for you, without spending a penny in advertising?

This is possible by building a network of resellers.

The simplest and most important distributor to approach is Amazon.

Simply create an account on Amazon Advantage (https://www.amazon.com/gp/seller-account/mm-product-page.html?topic=200329780) and provide the information related to your product.

It's an interesting solution if your product is a physical product such as a paper book or DVD.

First you can send one or two copies, then you could later increase the number and send your products by dozens as your product starts to sell well and you have good reviews.

If your product is 100% digital, you can make it available on affiliate platforms.

If people like it, you can literally build an army of affiliates who will sell your product for you in exchange of a commission generally ranging between 10% and 75% (each affiliate platform allows you to choose the commission percentage you want to give your affiliates, in a range that is specific to each platform).

The higher the commission paid to your affiliates is, the more affiliates you will attract to promote your product.

The largest Internet platform specialized in digital products is Clickbank (http://www.clickbank.com).

There are a multitude of other interesting platforms, such as JVZoo (http://www.jvzoo.com) who is a rising value and perceived as offering quality products.

By searching well, you will certainly find an affiliate platform corresponding to your needs.

VI- CREATE YOUR BLOG AND A COMMUNITY OF FANS (7 JOURS).

One of the fastest ways to get targeted and massive quality traffic is certainly what we saw in the previous chapter by the cost per click advertisement.

But you can choose to have another source of traffic, this time not by paying with money but with time.

The idea is to create a place that will serve you as a basis, and where you can share your expertise and promote your product and all the new one you create.

It consists in creating your blog.

Indeed, now that you've managed to create a business that works with the previous pages and that make you earn money, you also have to think about your development over time, and build a blog is a great way to do it.

We are going to see in the following pages how to set up your blog and start it, so that it makes you a strong foundation that will allow you to project yourself and develop your business in the long term.

VI.1- How To Think Your Blog.

There are two ways to think your blog.

The first way is all about satisfying your ego and showing that you are "the one who knows." This strategy is already a lost battle because it will never make you win money.

The second is to think of your blog as a business. In other words, to remove everything that is unnecessary and to concentrate on strategies that can allow you to make money.

The three main goals of a blog should be, in order of importance:

1- Increasing the number of subscribers to your mailing list.

2. Increasing the number of fans on social networks (Facebook and Twitter).

3- Selling you products.

Remove everything else that doesn't serve these three goals. We are going to detail each on of these three goals in the following pages.

VI.2- Increase The Number Of Subscribers To Your Mailing List.

Increasing the number of subscribers to your mailing list is by far the most important goal of your blog, because it is in your list that lies the money (or at least in the value you deliver to your list, as Franck Kern use to say).

Having a list of subscribers is the best way to ensure stability and continuity for your business.

Once you have a new product to offer, you simply need to create a small sequence of three or four emails delivered automatically through your autoresponder, with a link to the offer you promote.

The conversion rate is usually very high because these people have subscribed themselves because they wanted more information or because they like what you do.

This way, it gives you stability and the guarantee of a regular stream of income over time.

So, put subscription forms to your mailing list at strategic locations in your blog.

What works best is often between the article title and the body of the article.

You can also try to put the form at the end of your articles.

As for your sales page, make split tests using Google Analytics to identify the best places in your blog where to put your subscription forms, and to test several different headlines to grab attention.

To make your visitors want to sign up, your forms will have to give a good reason to take action and leave their email address.

It may be by promising them to regularly receive tips or advices, or by offering them a gift that will be sent for free to their email address.

Don't forget to use quality emailing platforms such as those mentioned in the IV.6 (Aweber, Getresponse, Icontact).

Concerning the style of your emails, customize them to the maximum, for example by using tags that display the name of your subscribers in the message.

Your email must give the impression that it is written specifically to the person who receives it.

Replacing overly formal sentences with more spontaneous expressions like "oh yeah, I forgot to tell you" or "talk soon" will contribute to give the impression of personalization.

Concerning the content of your emails, it should not be promotional, and I suggest you do not try to sell anything inside it.

The only thing you need to sell in an email is the click to a link. Use curiosity and awaken the interest of your readers so they will want to click on it.

These links should not systematically redirect to the sales pages of your products, but also to free content you put on your blog or your Youtube channel, such as your articles or videos.

Alternate regularly your emails: some with links to free content, others with links to paid content.

For example, send a sequence of two emails with links sending visitors to your free content, then an email with links sending to the sales page of one of your products, or to an affiliate product you're promoting. Then repeat.

Remember that you will first have to build a trusting relationship with your readers. And the worst way to do it would be to bombard them immediately and exclusively with promotions.

This is absolutely not what they expected to receive from you when they subscribed, and remember to always give before receiving, by offering free and relevant information before promoting your products.

This is not only essential to not scare away your subscribers, but also it will help you pre-sell your products by increasing interest and by demonstrating your expertise, without saying the whole story.

VI.3- Increase The Number Of Fans On Social Networks.

The second goal is to increase the number of fans on social networks.

There is a double advantage to it:

On one hand, having many fans will give you an important social proof that you can display on your blog using a social widget, which will give your site credibility.

On the other hand, having many fans also means a potential higher number of social shares and thus increase the visibility of your blog.

Facebook and Twitter are the two major social networks on which I advise you to spend time.

According to the audience you want to target, you can focus more on one than the other.

Facebook attracts a more generalist audience, while Twitter attracts more an audience related to computers, the Internet or technologies.

Regarding the animation strategy of these social networks, I advise you to systematically share a link to any new article you post on your blog.

This strategy will be very effective to create traffic to your blog which will provide relevant information.

But do not only post links to your articles. Use these social networks to publish interesting content in order to build trust with your subscribers and get more shares, allowing you to increase your visibility.

However as explained above, do not try to sell your products on social networks.

You would make people run away since they are not on social media to buy anything but mostly to spend time with their friends and play.

VI.4- Sell Your Products.

The third goal is to use your blog to sell and promote your products.

Of course you shouldn't only do this. Selling your products should fit into an overall strategy in which you will create high-quality content through written articles, podcasts or videos that you will give your readers relevant, useful and free, information, but without saying the whole story.

The purpose of your articles is to teach something to your readers, to motivate them, to make them dream, to inspire them, or to share your thoughts. You should awaken in them the desire to know more and to buy your product to go to the next level.

For example, if your blog is about seduction, you'll give relevant advices on how to approach a girl in various places, on the way to perfectly manage a first date etc, but you will remain general and won't go too deep into details as you do in your product.

The articles of your blog should make you appear as an expert by providing relevant and useful information through the high-quality content, or at least as someone who has something interesting and useful to share.

At the end of each free article, you can put for example a list of products related to the article, for people who would like to go one step further.

Or you can put at the end of the article a button such as "click here to go much further," and that will lead the reader to the sales page of your product.

Finally, it is important to choose a publication frequency that respects your time and that is high enough not to make visitors forget about you.

Indeed, the regularity of publication is essential to build your audience.

Try to publish at least one article a week, but do not publish an article a day if you do not have time.

It's much better to publish one or two good articles in the week that make you look like an expert or like someone people like to follow because of the information you share or the way you share it, rather than five articles per week that make you look like a fool.

Finally, forecast to have one to two weeks of articles in advance in case you have something unexpected.

Using the Wordpress platform (https://www.wordpress.org/) to create your blog is certainly the best way, and it will allow you to write several articles in advance and plan their publication without the need to do it manually.

VII- LAST RECOMMENDATIONS.

If you have completed all the steps in this book, then you are already on your way to financial independence on the Internet.

Your campaigns will become profitable and you will have built a strategy enabling you to develop your business in a stable manner and over the long term.

Remember though to regularly optimize all your campaigns.

For that, plan two hours a week during which you will check the performance of your different ads, keywords, sales pages, and take the opportunity to create new ads and new split tests to replace those which gave the lowest results.

Never miss this weekly meeting because it is essential for the sustainability of your business.

Also, create new products regularly in the same topic, and don't promote only one product.

It will increase the average shopping cart per customer and your sales will no longer be limited to a single product, especially for existing clients that are a real goldmine and who would certainly love to buy something else from you.

Indeed, it is much easier to make an existing customer buy again from you than it is to make a prospect buy for the first time.

The reason is that an existing customer already knows your sales process and also the value your product brought him. He is no longer in an unknown territory and he trusts you for the upcoming products.

That's why I recommend you to stay in the same topic, because the audience and the customers you have acquired will be specially interested in products that complement those they have already purchased, and not in products that have nothing to do with the topic.

The idea is to create a product that is complete enough to satisfy the customer, but then to propose inside this same product a complementary product to go further into details on a particular aspect.

For example, if your product is about learning how to play accompaniment guitar, you can then offer a complementary product on how to learn solo guitar or how to learn famous songs.

The simple fact of dividing a very complete product into two or more smaller and cheaper products can significantly increase the average expense spent per customer.

Thus, you can regularly offer new products that your existing customers would be happy to buy, and that will increase even more your revenue.

VIII- CONCLUSION.

By putting into practice the advices I shared with you in these pages, you have right now the possibility to create an Internet business partially automated, and to achieve financial and geographical independence.

Of course, you may find there are a lot of things to digest in one go, but it really worth starting and persevering.

Now that you know the right principles, you just need to take action and enjoy the rest of your life with more time for you, for your family and your passions.

Having your business on the Internet is an incredible opportunity to realize your dreams, and finally be free to lead your life exactly as you want it.

No boss to dictate what you should or shouldn't do, and no fixed schedules where you must absolutely be present.

That being said, freedom also often means responsibility. For many people, it is not easy to accept losing the hypothetic security of being employed in a company to start a personal business and to be finally free.

It's all a question of self-confidence, of believing in your capacities to create your own independence. And nothing prevents you from starting your personal business in parallel of your employed work.

The job security is almost always what refrains many people from taking action, what keeps them away from living their dreams, far much more than the passion and pleasure people have in their daily work.

However, this security is completely illusory, because anyone can be fired at any time of his life, even when someone decide to build his whole life plan around his work and serve his company, and then end up by being coldly thanked and fired overnight, after 25 years of his life wasted to serve the interests of the company.

I didn't wanted anymore this model of career because it didn't correspond me anymore.

This is also why I wanted to share with you in these pages the strategies that allowed me to walk away from that model and create my financial independence, so that you too can become free to live the way you want and have the life you dream of.

Remember : life is short, and we only have one.

IX- ABOUT THE AUTHOR.

Remy Roulier is a former computer engineer and marketing manager in a multinational company.

He is now a best-selling author, digital nomad and he travels all around the world, having acquired for over ten years a real expertise in Internet marketing and personal development.

He now shares his tools and experience to allow others to also achieve financial independence and shape their life the way they really want.

X- MORE BOOKS FROM THE SAME AUTHOR.

HOW TO CONCENTRATE LIKE EINSTEIN:
THE LAZY STUDENT'S WAY TO INSTANTLY IMPROVE MEMORY & GRADES
WITH THE DOCTOR VITTOZ SECRET CONCENTRATION TECHNIQUE

Concentrate now on what you want as long as you want by learning the never before revealed concentration technique used by Einstein.

RESCUE ACUPRESSURE:
INSTANTLY SUPPRESS STRESS, HEADACHES, MEMORY LAPSES IN
DESPERATE SITUATIONS LIKE DURING AN EXAM

Relieve pain and discomfort immediately when you need it and do not let them make you fail an exam, a job interview or any important moment of your life. 100% practical, very clear and simple, this book is definitely the best investment you can do for your health and success.

www.ingramcontent.com/pod-product-compliance
Lightning Source LLC
Chambersburg PA
CBHW070255190526
45169CB00001B/424